D1511056

JOMO

EMBRACE THE JOY OF MISSING OUT

CREATED + ILLUSTRATED BY KATE POCRASS

CHRONICLE BOOKS
SAN FRANCISCO

HERE WE ARE:

OVEREXTENDED, UNDER-FULFILLED, AND READY FOR A SHAKE UP. LET'S TAKE STOCK SHALL WE?

I TEND to DO THE FOLLOWING:

- ☐ INSTINCTUALLY SCROLL THROUGH SOCIAL MEDIA WHILE WAITING IN LINE
- ☐ REPLY TO EMAILS IMMEDIATELY AFTER RECEIVING THEM
- ☐ RSVP "YES" TO ALL EXTENDED INVITATIONS
- ☐ POST ABOUT THE FOOD I EAT AND WHO I'M WITH
- ☐ FOCUS MORE ON THE PHOTO OP THAN THE EXPERIENCE I'M HAVING
- ☐ HAVE ANXIETY ABOUT MISSING OUT

WHAT I REALLY WANT IS:

- ☐ TO DELIGHT IN THE MOMENT
- ☐ TO CHECK OUT FROM OTHERS AND CHECK IN WITH MYSELF
- ☐ PERMISSON TO LAZILY DAYDREAM
- ☐ REAL CONNECTION INSTEAD OF VIRTUAL APPROVAL
- ☐ TO EXPLORE WITHOUT THE PRESSURE TO POST ABOUT IT
- ☐ TO FEEL CONTENT DOING THINGS SOLO

ALRIGHT THEN,
WHERE to START?

STEP **1** DISMISS NERVOUSNESS AND EMBRACE THIS JOURNAL

STEP **2** TAKE STOCK OF YOUR HABITS AND SET YOUR INTENTIONS

STEP **3** TRY OUT THE PROMPTS FOR STAYING IN (ORDER IS NOT AT ALL IMPORTANT)

STEP **4** GO OUT AND ABOUT ON UNPLUGGED ADVENTURES (IN THE BACKYARD OR MILES AWAY)

STEP **5** JOT DOWN THOUGHTS, INSIGHTS, AND IDEAS ALONG THE WAY

STEP AWAY FROM YOUR ROUTINE, MAKE THE CONSCIOUS CHOICE TO DISCONNECT, AND EMBRACE THE JOY OF MISSING OUT. THUMB THROUGH THESE PAGES AND FIND CREATIVE SUGGESTIONS TO SHIFT FROM VIEWING TO DOING, AND GAIN MORE TIME IN YOUR DAY FOR THE GOOD STUFF.

READY?
IT'S TIME.

SET YOUR INTENTIONS

	MONDAY	TUESDAY	WEDNESDA.

FILL IN

KEEP TRACK OF YOUR SOCIAL MEDIA TIME FOR ONE WEEK

THURSDAY	FRIDAY	SATURDAY	SUNDAY

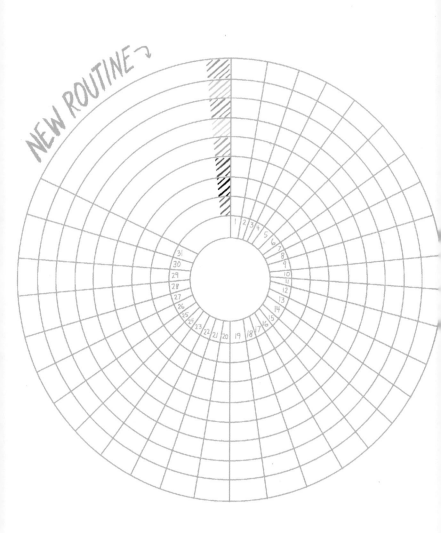

NEW ROUTINE ↵

CREATE NEW ROUTINES

1. _____
2. _____
3. _____
4. _____
5. _____
6. _____
7. _____
8. _____

FILL IN THE CIRCULAR TRACKER FOR ONE MONTH TO SEE WHICH HABITS YOU ARE EMBRACING

DINNER
IN BED

REASONS YOU LOVE STAYING HOME

Chicago History Museum

WMAA

M

The Morgan

D I A

Dia:

GOING
TO A
MUSEUM

MÜTTER MUSEUM

MIT MUSIC & THEATER ARTS MTA

Georgia
O'Keeffe
Museum

TheNew
Museum

K

Musées de Strasbourg

ACTIVITIES YOU LOVE DOING SOLO

YUBA RIVER

PLACES TO CHECK OUT ON YOUR NEXT SOLO ADVENTURES

CROSS-STITCH

ANALOG PLEASURES

G5RV

W5OGK

KA1ME

W6CLZ

HAM RADIO
OPERATOR

G6BW

U-8CRF
RADIO SOCIETY

VE5JL

NEW HOBBIES YOU WANT TO TRY

REPOT PLANTS

MEND BUTTONS

MAKE KOMBUCHA

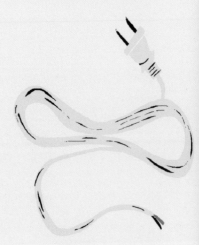

REWIRE LAMP

PROJECTS YOU WANT
TO STAY HOME AND TACKLE

I HEREBY WILL NOT
CALL HOME WHILE:

LISTENING
TO A PODCAST
FOLDING THE LAUNDRY
COOKING DINNER
WAITING FOR FILES
TO UPLOAD
SCROLLING TWITTER

THINGS YOU SHOULD
SLOW DOWN AND SINGLE-TASK

LOVED IT ★★★★★

WASTE OF TIME ★☆☆☆☆

MOVIES TO SEE AND
SHOWS TO BINGE-WATCH

BOOKS TO READ THIS YEAR

CLEANING OUT
THE DRYER LINT

MUNDANE TASKS YOU LOVE

WATERING
THE PLANTS

ORDINARY MOMENTS
YOU REVEL IN

GIVE YOURSELF KUDOS FOR...

_____

_____

_____

_____

_____

_____

_____

_____

_____

_____

_____

_____

_____

_____

_____

_____

_____

_____

_____

_____

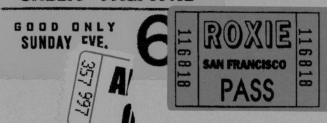

SEC. B LEFT CENTR ROW X SEAT 45

GREEK THEATRE

GOOD ONLY SUNDAY EVE.

6

357 997

ROXIE SAN FRANCISCO PASS 116818 116818

AD

12813 ADM ONI

TAKE YOURSELF TO A SHOW

13711 ADM ONE

WAYS TO TREAT YOURSELF

"EVERY DAY MAY NOT BE GOOD... BUT THERE'S SOMETHING GOOD IN EVERY DAY."

—ALICE MORSE EARLE

SPACE FOR GOOD THOUGHTS

WHAT I WANT TO CHANGE AND HOW I WILL CHANGE IT

SPACE FOR VENTING

FLY-FISHING

NEW EXPERIENCES
YOU WANT TO HAVE

PINK SOFA

TRENDS YOU ARE
HAPPY YOU DID NOT ADOPT

OFFICE
HAPPY HOUR

THINGS YOU
WANT TO SAY "NO" TO

SHOW GRACE
DON'T IGNORE
REPLY PROMPTLY
BE FIRM
BE HONEST
BE THANKFUL
BE BRIEF

WAYS TO DECLINE AN EVENT

WANDER AROUND TOGETHER

GRAB A COFFEE

TAKE A DAY TRIP

CHAT ON A STOOP

PEOPLE TO REACH OUT TO
IRL IN THE COMING MONTH

THINK ABOUT THIS PAST WEEK.

LIST WAYS YOU COULD HAVE DONE THINGS DIFFERENTLY TO FREE UP YOUR SCHEDULE.

20

PHONE CHECK

№ 20

PHONE CHECK CLAIM TICKET

HOST IS NOT RESPONSIBLE FOR
ANXIETY CAUSED BY BEING
FULLY PRESENT AND ENGAGING IN
FREE-FLOWING CONVERSATION.

HAVE A DINNER PARTY AND CHECK
EVERYONE'S PHONES IN AT THE DOOR.
NOTE ANY CHANGES IN CONVERSATION.

DRAW A SELF-PORTRAIT
INSTEAD OF TAKING A SELFIE

WATER

MEAT

SKIN

HUSK

IS A COCONUT A NUT?

DEBATE AND WRITE ANSWERS TO
QUESTIONS WITHOUT LOOKING
THEM UP ON YOUR PHONE

FIND SOMETHING THAT IS
BEAUTIFUL TO YOU.
WRITE ABOUT IT.
KEEP IT TO YOURSELF.

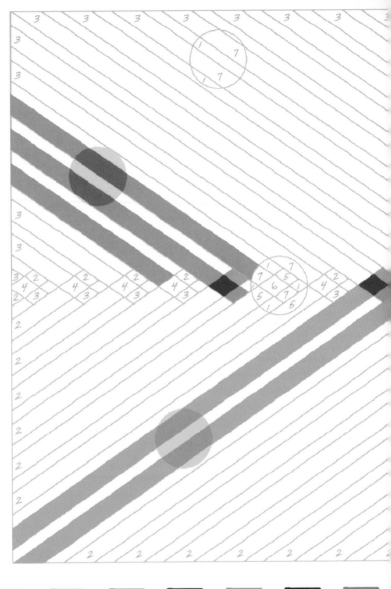

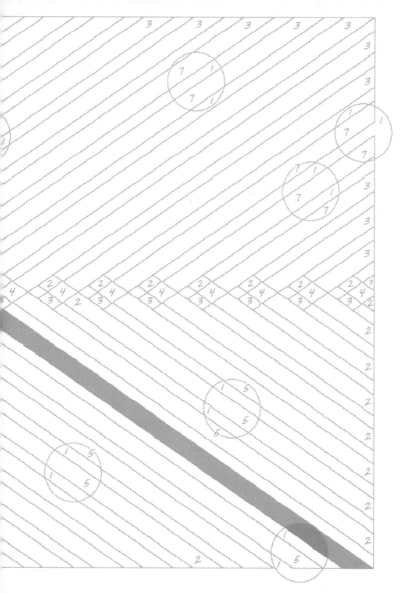

DO SOMETHING MINDLESS. PAINT BY NUMBERS.

MEANDER THROUGH
THE PARK
DRIVE AT A
SLOWER PACE
TAKE THE NON-
EXPRESS BUS
GET OFF BEFORE
YOUR USUAL STOP

TAKE THE LONG WAY HOME.
NAME ONE THING YOU SAW ANEW.

FIRST PERSON TO CHECK THEIR PHONE
WHILE AT A RESTAURANT FOOTS THE BILL

WHO
HAD TO PAY:

TIME IT TOOK
FOR THEM
TO BREAK

ARD
'S TO DO?

___ ___ : ___ ___
MIN   SEC

NO PAIN   TOLERABLE   DISCOMFORTING   DISTRESSING   INTENSE   HORRIBLE   UNBEARABLE

PICK A DAY OF THE WEEK TO STAY ON "DO NOT DISTURB" MODE. REFLECT ON HOW YOU FEEL AFTERWARD.

TIME _____
LOCATION _____

TIME _____
LOCATION _____

TIME _____
LOCATION _____

TIME _____
LOCATION _____

TIME _____
LOCATION _____

TIME _____
LOCATION _____

STORYBOARD
YOUR MORNING
AND DOCUMENT
TIME PASSING

TIME _____
LOCATION _____

TAKE A SMALL SOLO
ADVENTURE TO LISTEN TO NATURE.

WHAT DO YOU HEAR?

PERSON	SUGGESTION
· A FRIEND'S PARENTS	
· CORNER STORE CLERK	
· STRANGER OVER SEVENTY	
· PERSON IN THEIR TWENTIES	
· YOUR HAIRDRESSER	

RATHER THAN LOOKING UP STAR RATINGS, ASK UNEXPECTED PEOPLE FOR RESTAURANT SUGGESTIONS

TURN
NOTIFICATIONS
OFF

DELETE
TIME-SUCKING
APPS

UNFOLLOW ACCOUNTS
THAT DON'T BRING
YOU HAPPINESS

DOWNSIZE YOUR TECH

UNSUBSRIBE
FROM EMAIL
LISTS

SET A TIMER WHEN
YOU CHECK IN
TO SOCIAL MEDIA

TAKE A NAP
READ IN THE PARK
WRITE IN A CAFE
PET THE CAT
SWING IN A
HAMMOCK
LISTEN TO A FULL
ALBUM

DESCRIBE YOUR PERFECT LAZY DAY. GIVE YOURSELF PERMISSION TO BE IDLE.

ZONE OUT WITH A WORD SEARCH

ANALOG
COMPARE-ITIS
CONTENT
DAYDREAM
DELIGHT
DETOUR
DISCONNECT
DOWNSIZE
FULFILLMENT
IDLE
INTENTIONAL
IRL
JOMO
OFFLINE
REBALANCE
SINGLE-TASK
SOLO
UNBURDEN
UNFOLLOW
UNPLUGGED
UNSUBSCRIBE

```
                              Q
                        E   Q W
                     G  G   W J
                  G  G  F   J S
               C  L  P  I   S T
               O  P  R  I   T O
            O  V  R  O  M   O T
            D  N  C  N  E   T X
            A  T  N  C  E   X T
         L  V  K  S  E  N   T E
         W  T  S  I  N  N   E G
         S  S  P  M  W  G   G V
            M  Q  D  W  V
            E  Q  X  G  G
            U  C  Y  X   K
               C  F  X   K S
               E  N  G   S H
                  G  P   H A
                  S  H   A J
                     N   J E
                         E H
                             H
```

```
      U U E
R J  H G L L D H
I L  N E C Z D J V G
E A X S Q T E I A W R X
L E K O S H T U V K K D C
B Z T L F U G I Y X U K W Q
V I K O T D Q C S Z T V T G
  S H D F L     A Y V C W V
  N D G Z O     N A Y E B A
Z W O P K J C O Q A B E N E U Z
U O O F U L F I L L M E N T N M
L D W N S O X R A O M W O O S W
J I U G U Y I X M G T G C T U Q T
S K N M Q A U T N X Q H S W B L E
A B Z E J G O R S O I J I O S T J
L Y J U S K I R C R H   D L C W
I T I E R A P M O C     Q L R X
G J Y H S T B E V       H J O I E
                        U O P F B
                        Q R M Y N E
T G L C M F A S B T G O R U
G G U L P N U R K M W J D Z
N U T Y S J S Y W G G K Z
Q I Z P M A E R D Y A D
T D E L I G H T G X
H E U K M Q N U
  D P C
```

LOOK AT CLOUDS
PLAY "I SPY" PEOPLE WATCH
NOTE ARCHITECTURE
CHAT INSPECT FOLIAGE

WAIT IN PEACE.
AVOID FILLING TIME
SCROLLING THROUGH FEEDS.

SET OUT FOR A
DEVICE-FREE WALK.

HOW IS THE EXPERIENCE DIFFERENT?

FIND SOMETHING INSIDE A MAGAZINE OR NEWSPAPER THAT REMINDS YOU OF A SPECIFIC FRIEND. MAIL THEM THE CLIPPING.

FOREVER

HI THERE.

WRITE A TO-DO LIST FOR THE WEEKEND. CROSS OFF HALF OF IT. FOCUS ON WHAT'S IMPORTANT AND LET GO OF THE REST.

75¢

75¢

$2

75¢

$5

50¢

$3

$1

$5

75¢

$3

$5

$2

CHAT WITH
THE CASHIER

READ THE
COMMUNITY
BULLETIN

BREAK YOUR RUSH.
LET DISTRACTION HAPPEN.

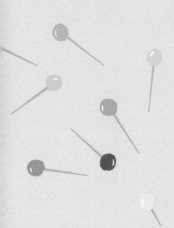

GET A SHOE SHINE

WATCH A SUNSET.
DESCRIBE IT IN WORDS.

ARRANGE
SOME LEAVES

MAKE A BRACELET

TAKE THIRTY MINUTES A DAY TO BE "UNPRODUCTIVE"

SKIP ROCKS

TAKE SOME TIME TO MEMORIZE A MOMENT.
RESIST THE URGE TO PHOTOGRAPH IT.
DRAW IT FROM MEMORY
LATER THAT EVENING.

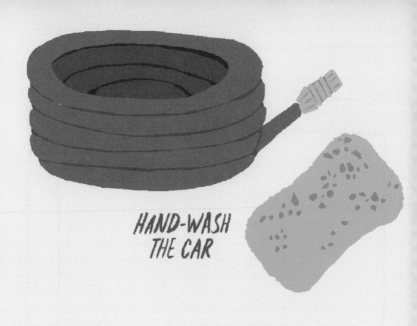

HAND-WASH
THE CAR

WASH DISHES SLOWLY

EMBRACE THE ART OF SLOWNESS

FOLD THE
LAUNDRY
METICULOUSLY

WRITE A REVIEW
ONLY YOU WILL SEE

RESTAURANT

☆☆☆☆☆ TASTE   ☆☆☆☆☆ SERVICE

PRODUCT

☆☆☆☆☆ PACKAGING   ☆☆☆☆☆ USAGE

MOVIE / BOOK

☆☆☆☆☆ WRITING ☆☆☆☆☆ VISUAL

GALLERY

☆☆☆☆☆ WORK ☆☆☆☆☆ AMBIANCE

TAKE A FEW MINUTES TO SOLVE A MAZE

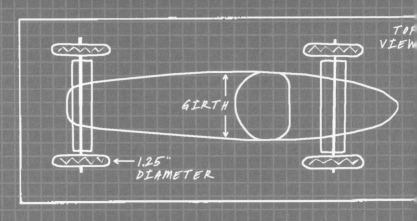

TOP
VIEW

GIRTH

← 1.25"
DIAMETER

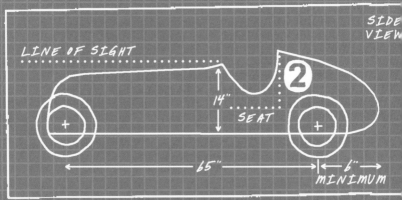

SIDE
VIEW

LINE OF SIGHT

14"

SEAT

②

65"

6"
MINIMUM

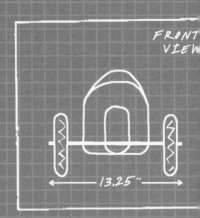

FRONT
VIEW

13.25"

BUILDING A
SOAP BOX CAR

MAKE TIME FOR
OBSCURE INTERESTS

☐

☐

☐

☐

☐

☐

☐

☐

☐

☐

PLAY A GAME OF SOLITAIRE
OR SOLVE A PUZZLE

IRL
BINGO

THE COLOR YELLOW	SKATE-BOARDER	RAIN CLOUD	BEE	NEWSPAPER
SIGN	PERSON LAUGHING	SHELL	FLOCK OF BIRDS	BALLOON
SAFETY CONE	CUP OF COFFEE	FREE SPOT	CYCLIST	PEOPLE SHOWING LOVE
BUS	ARCHED WINDOW	FERN	GREEN CAR	ANIMAL
SOMETHING FLUFFY	FLAG	OCTAGON	THE LETTER "P"	WATER

STARE OUT THE WINDOW. DESCRIBE WHAT YOU SEE.

GOOD

RECORD ALL THE GOOD THIN

1

2

3

4

NEWS

IT HAPPENED THIS WEEK

5

6

7

"COMPARISON IS
THE THIEF
OF JOY."
– THEODORE ROOSEVELT

FOCUS ON YOURSELF
INSTEAD OF
EVERYONE ELSE

THERE
IS POWER IN
NOT CARING
WHAT OTHER PEOPLE
ARE UP TO

STOP BEING AVAILABLE TO UNAVAILABLE PEOPLE

WHEN YOU DON'T FEEL
LIKE YOU ARE MISSING OUT,
YOU AREN'T

"TO BE YOURSELF IN A WORLD THAT IS CONSTANTLY TRYING TO MAKE YOU SOMETHING ELSE IS THE GREATEST ACCOMPLISHMENT.

-RALPH WALDO EMERSON

DELIGHT IN THE MOMENT
AND DISCONNECT

FIND HAPPINESS
IN BEING WHERE YOU ARE

TAKE TIME
TO DO NOTHING
AND DO IT WITH

PURPOSE

EMBRACE IDLENESS

LET GO OF
THE SHOULDS

"BEWARE OF
THE BARRENNESS
OF A BUSY LIFE."

-SOCRATES

MAKE THE
RADICAL CHOICE
TO SLOW
DOWN

LET GO
OF THE COMPULSION
TO DO IT ALL

DO *MORE* THINGS
THAT MAKE YOU
FORGET
YOUR
PHONE

LIFE DOESN'T HAVE TO LOOK PERFECT TO BE PERFECT

"WHATEVER LIFTS
THE CORNERS
OF YOUR MOUTH,
TRUST THAT."

-RUMI

UNBURDEN YOURSELF. FIND FREEDOM IN OPTING OUT.

CONNECT WITH YOURSELF

YOURSELF

AS MUCH AS YOU
CONNECT TO WI-FI

YOU DON'T HAVE TO
POST CONTENT TO
BE CONTENT

"SAYING NOTHING SOMETIMES SAYS THE MOST."

-EMILY DICKINSON

THERE IS
NO FILTER
FOR CONTENTMENT

YOU DON'T HAVE TO
BE AN INFLUENCER
TO BE A
GOOD INFLUENCE

YOUR REVOLUTION WILL NOT BE INSTAGRAMMED

DON'T REFRESH YOUR FEED
TO FEEL FED

LET GO
OF BEING
IN THE KNOW

THE FAKE GRASS IS ALWAYS GREENER

WE ONLY HAVE 24 HOURS IN A DAY. WHAT DO YOU WANT TO FILL THEM WITH?

REBALANCE
YOUR PRIORITIES

CHOOSE YOUR
OWN STORY